Take off with

SHAPE

Take off with

SHAPE

Sally Hewitt

Evans

Evans Brothers Limited

About this book

The activities, puzzles and games in this book about shape have been designed for an adult and child to enjoy together. Take a while over the pages and enjoy finding out the many opportunities they provide for learning about shape and how we recognise it.

Each page deals with a topic that children will be introduced to in the early years at school. The pictures are of familiar objects and everyday situations that will help children to realise that shape is not just about lines and corners, but that it is an important part of life.

The games and activities in the 'Take Off' loops will give children a chance to practise and develop the new skills they have been introduced to on that page. Children learn most effectively by joining in, talking, asking questions and solving problems, so encourage them to talk about what they are doing and to find ways of solving the problems for themselves.

Use the book as a starting point. Look for other opportunities to learn about shape, for example, pointing out shapes when you are looking at picture books, discussing the shapes they see in a supermarket or encouraging them to use shapes in their painting and craft activities. Make sure that it is not only easy to take off with shape but also fun!

Contents

Shapes everywhere

There are shapes all around us.
Here are some flat shapes.
Can you name any of them?

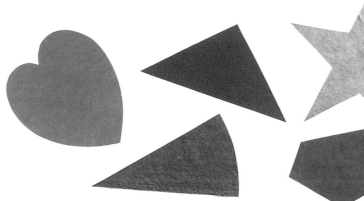

You can draw flat shapes.

You can print them.

You can cut them out.

Look out for flat shapes
on things you see around.

Not all shapes are flat –
everything has a shape.
All these things are
solid shapes.

Here are the same things again.
Can you tell what they are whichever way
you look at them?

Spot the curved lines, the straight lines,
the corners, twists and points.
Look out for flat shapes as well.

Feely bag

Collect some small objects
and put them in a bag.

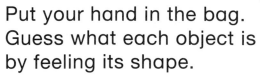

Put your hand in the bag.
Guess what each object is
by feeling its shape.

Ask a friend to do the same
thing and guess as well.

Circles

Put your finger on the edge
of this circle and move it round
and round the curved line.

All these shapes are circles.

Point out all the circular shapes
you can spot here.

Try drawing a circle.
Can you make it perfectly round?

You can draw around
circular objects to make
circles – and circle patterns.

Why do you think
wheels are circular?

Imagine what would
happen if they had
straight lines and corners!

Spheres

A sphere is a perfectly round ball shape.
Its curved surface is always the same whichever way you turn it.

These are all spheres.
They are very good for rolling, throwing and hitting.

All these things are sphere shaped.
But they are not all perfectly round.

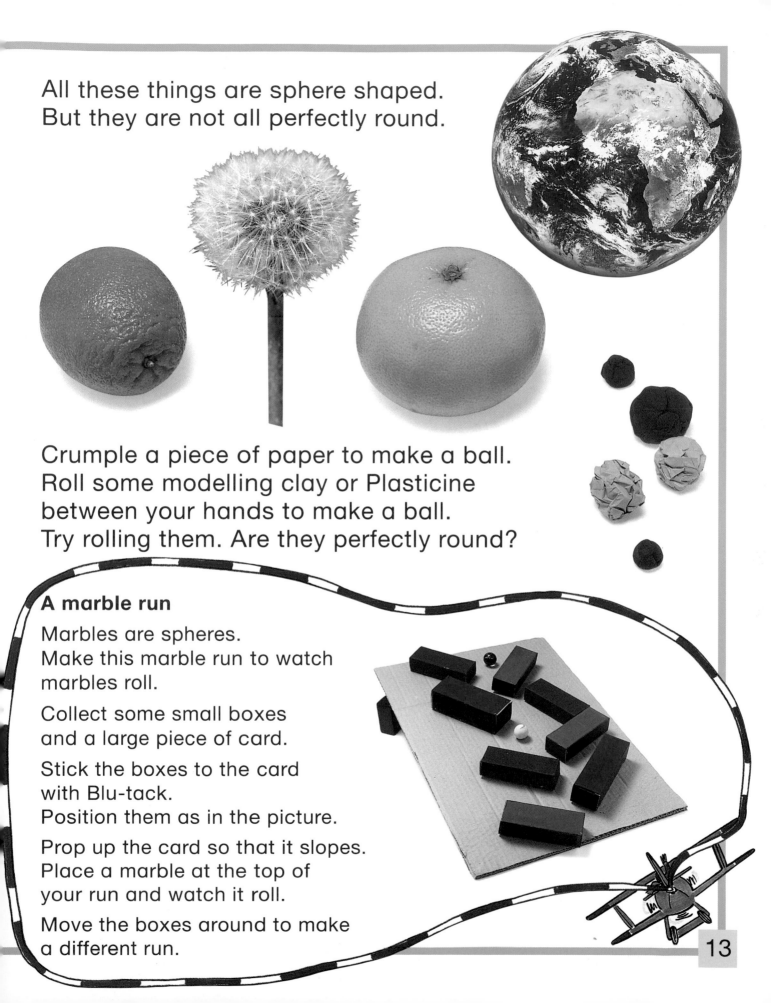

Crumple a piece of paper to make a ball.
Roll some modelling clay or Plasticine
between your hands to make a ball.
Try rolling them. Are they perfectly round?

A marble run

Marbles are spheres.
Make this marble run to watch
marbles roll.

Collect some small boxes
and a large piece of card.

Stick the boxes to the card
with Blu-tack.
Position them as in the picture.

Prop up the card so that it slopes.
Place a marble at the top of
your run and watch it roll.

Move the boxes around to make
a different run.

13

Squares

A square has 4 sides all exactly the same length.
It has 4 corners.
Corners are also called angles.

Each inside corner of a square is the same size.
It is called a right angle.

A right angle checker

Make a right angle checker with a scrap of paper.

Fold the paper in half to make a straight edge.
Fold it in half again along this edge.

The corner you have made is a right angle.

Which of these shapes are squares?
Measure the sides with a ruler.
Are they all the same length?

Fit the right angle checker into the corners.
Are they all right angles?

The answer is yes to both these questions for the red and the blue shapes.
These shapes are squares.

How many square shapes can you spot?

Squares tessellate.
This means they fit together
without any gaps between them.
Can you see any tessellating
square patterns?

Circles do not tessellate.
Can you see why?

Cubes

This is a cube.
It has 6 flat sides called faces.
You can only see 3 in the picture.
The faces are all the same size.

Each of this cube's
6 faces has been painted
a different colour.

The faces of the cube have been
pulled apart and laid out flat.
You can see that each one
is the same shape and size.

Count the faces.
What shape are they?
Use your ruler and right angle
checker to find out.

They are squares. Were you right?

Which one of these shapes is not a cube?

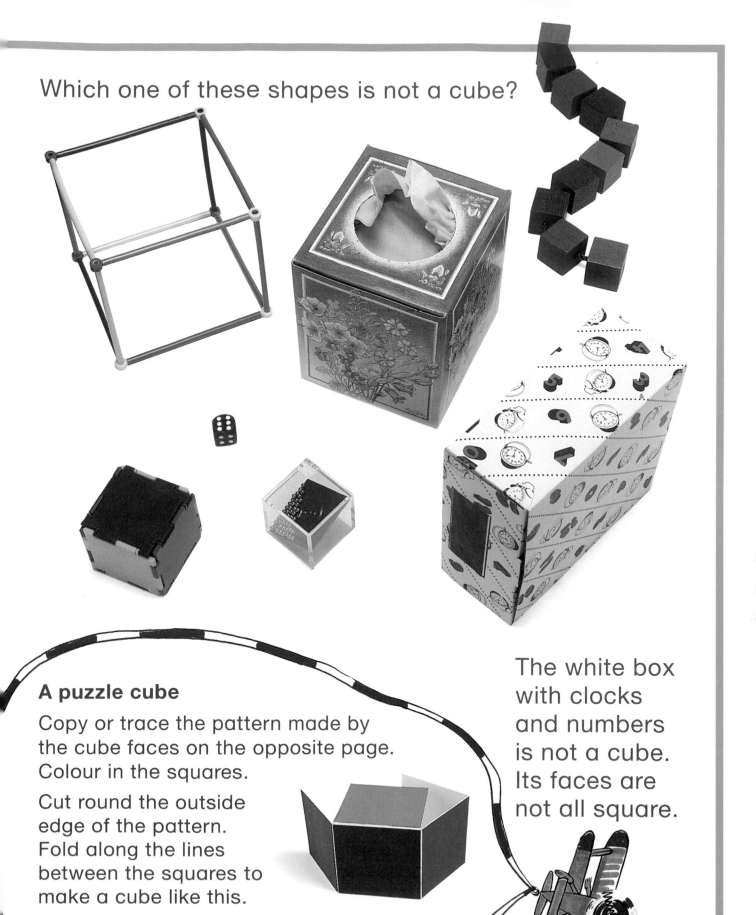

A puzzle cube

Copy or trace the pattern made by the cube faces on the opposite page. Colour in the squares.

Cut round the outside edge of the pattern. Fold along the lines between the squares to make a cube like this.

How quickly can you friends make a cube with your puzzle?

The white box with clocks and numbers is not a cube. Its faces are not all square.

Rectangles

A rectangle has
4 straight sides.
Each of the 2 pairs of
facing sides are the same length.
Its four corners are right angles.
A square is a special kind of rectangle.

Are these shapes all rectangles?
Measure the sides and check the corners
with your right angle checker.

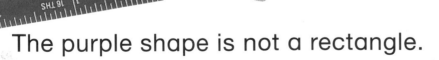

The purple shape is not a rectangle.

More and more rectangles

Fold a rectangle of paper in half,
then in half again and again until
it is a very small rectangle.

Open out the paper and colour in
all the new rectangles you have
made with the folds.

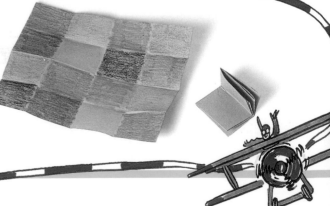

18

Look out for rectangular shapes
next time you walk down the street.

How many rectangular shapes can see
on this street?

Try drawing a picture
using only rectangles.

This dog is made of
rectangles.

Cuboids

This is a cuboid.
It has 6 rectangular
faces.

This is the same
cuboid standing on
a different face.

All these shapes are cuboids.

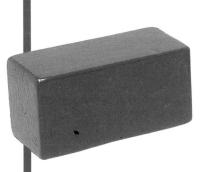

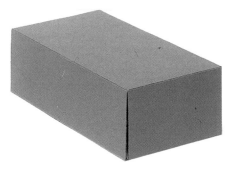

The purple box has been
opened out flat.
How many of its faces
are the same size?

Make faces

Find a cuboid box and open it
out. Cut off any flaps that are
keeping it together. Now cut off
the faces and paint them in
matching
pairs.

Where would each face appear
if you put the cuboid back
together again?

20

Cuboid shapes fit together very well. Cuboid boxes are easy to store and move.

Building bricks are cuboid shaped. Why do you think they are made this way?

Try building with some bricks. Put them together in different patterns.

What do you think would happen if you tried to build with spheres?

Triangles

Triangles have 3 straight sides and 3 corners.

These are all triangles.
Use a ruler to find which triangle has 3 sides all the same length.
Use your right angle checker to find which triangle has a right angle.

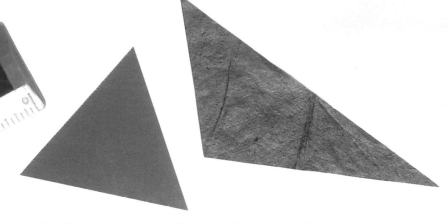

The pink triangle has 3 equal sides.
The red triangle has a right angle.
Were you right?

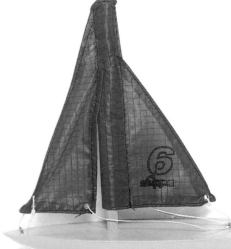

Spot the triangular shapes.

A triangle is a very strong shape. Triangles often support the roofs of houses.

Triangles give a strong support to bridges, too.

Drawing triangles

Make 3 dots on a piece of paper.

Join them up with straight lines to make a triangle.

Triangles will tessellate.

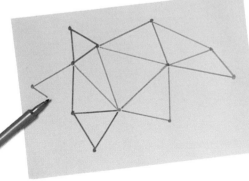

Now put another dot on the page. Join this to the two nearest corners of the triangle.
You have made a second triangle.

Keep on adding dots and joining them to your triangles.

Cut out a card triangle and draw round it to make patterns.

23

Pyramids and cones

This is a pyramid.
A pyramid is made up of triangle faces
that meet together in a point.
Another face joins together
the bottom end of the pyramid's
triangle faces.
This face is often the base of the pyramid.
It does not have to be a triangle.

Which of these pyramids have a square base?

The Egyptian pyramids are
famous pyramid shaped
buildings.

A cone is a bit like a pyramid.
It has a circle face
at one end and
a curved face that
makes a point at
the other.

Which of these things use a cone shape?

Make a cone

Draw round a large plate and cut out
the circle you make.

Fold the circle in half and in half again.
Open it out.

Cut along one of the fold lines until
you reach the point where it crosses
the other. This is the centre of the circle.

Pull one side of the cut over the other.
The circle will curl into a cone shape.
Stick down the edges.

Think of ways you can use your cone.

Cylinders

A cylinder has a circle
at each end.
They are joined together by
a curved face.
The cylinder is the same thickness
along the whole of its length.

If you match the colours you can find
which cylinder was used to print
which circle.

Cylinders are easy to make.
Roll up a rectangle of paper
and stick down the edge.

A cylinder is a very useful shape.
All these things make use of cylinders.
Which of them have to be able to roll?

Ready to roll

Find a sphere, a cone and a cylinder or use ones you have made. Try rolling them.

Which one can roll in every direction?

27

Polygons

A polygon is any flat shape
with three or more straight sides.

These are all polygons.

A triangle is a
polygon with 3 sides.

A pentagon is a
polygon with 5 sides.
Both these shapes
are pentagons.

A hexagon is a
polygon with 6 sides.

Can you name any others?
All the flat straight-sided shapes we
have looked at in this book are polygons.

Describe a shape

Put out some of the shapes you have cut out or made.

Choose a shape.
Don't point it out but describe it to a friend.
For example, it has 3 straight sides
and 3 corners.

Your friend must point to the shape
you have described.

These shapes are made from
lots of different polygons.

Which ones have triangle faces?
What other flat shapes can you see?

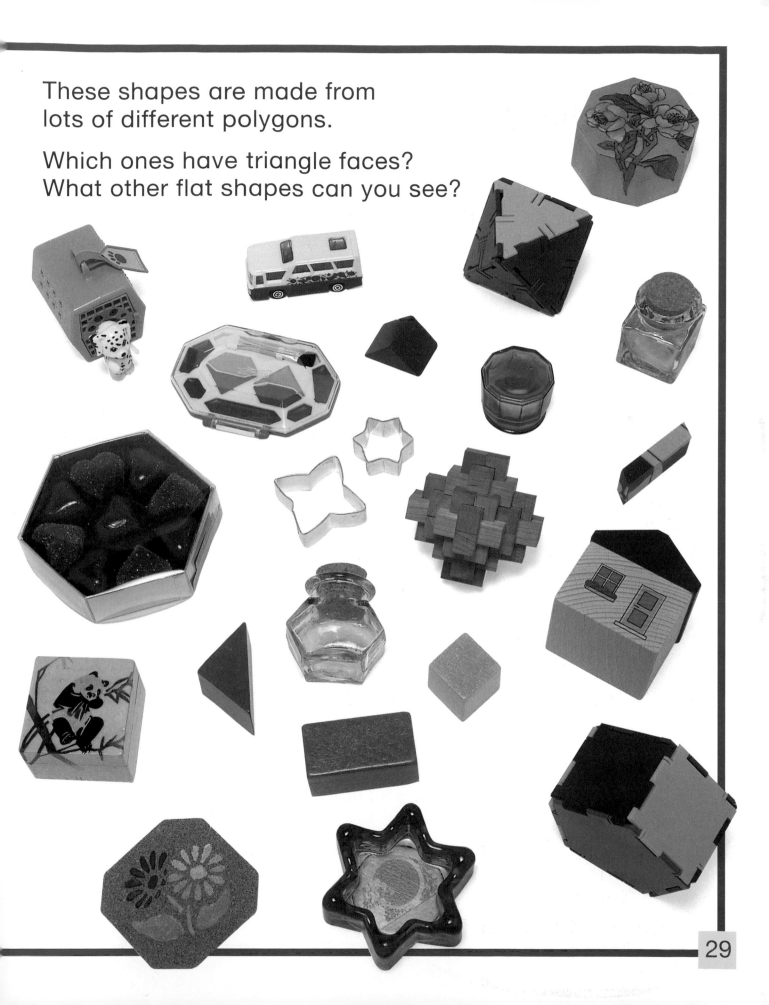